Animal Top Tens

Africa's Most Amazing Animals

Anita Ganeri

Chicago, Illinois

Photo Research: Mica Brancic
Editorial: Nancy Dickmann and Catherine Veitch
Design: Victoria Bevan and Geoff Ward
Illustrations: Geoff Ward
Production: Victoria Fitzgerald

Originated by Modern Age
Printed and bound by CTPS (China Translation
& Printing Services Ltd)

12 11 10 09 08
10 9 8 7 6 5 4 3 2 1

Library of Congress Cataloging-in-Publication Data

Ganeri, Anita, 1961-
  Africa's most amazing animals / Anita Ganeri.
    p. cm. -- (Animal top tens)
  Includes bibliographical references and index.
  ISBN 978-1-4109-3083-5 (hc) -- ISBN 978-1-4109-3092-7 (pb) 1. Animals--Africa--Juvenile literature. I. Title. II. Series.
QL336.G29 2008
591.96--dc22

                              2007047419

Acknowledgments
The author and publisher are grateful to the following for permission to reproduce copyright material: ©Ardea pp. 8 (Chris Harvey), 10 (M. Watson), 18 (Pat Morris); ©FLPA pp. 4 (Ariadne Van Zandbergen), 7 (Ariadne Van Zandbergen) [Ardea], 19 (David Hosking), 27 (Fritz Polking); ©FLPA/Minden Pictures pp. 20, 23; ©Naturepl pp. 13 (Bruce Davidson); ©NHPA p. 21 (Stephen Dalton); ©OSF pp. 6 (Francois Savigny), 9 (Tom Brakefield), 11 (Karl Ammann), 14 (Gallo Images-Anthony Bannister), 15 (Austin J. Stevens), 16, 17 (Dupc Dupc/David Haring), 22 (Roger De La Harpe), 24 (Patti Murray), 26 (Wisniewski Wisniewski).

Cover photograph of an aye-aye, reproduced with permission of OSF/David Haring/Dupc.

The publisher would like to thank Michael Bright for his assistance in the preparation of this book.

Every effort has been made to contact copyright holders of any material reproduced in this book. Any omissions will be rectified in subsequent printings if notice is given to the publisher.

Disclaimer
All the internet addresses (URLs) given in this book were valid at time of going to press. However, due to the dynamic nature of the Internet, some addresses may have changed, or sites may have changed or ceased to exist since publication. While the author and publishers regret any inconvenience this may cause readers, no responsibility for any such changes can be accepted by either the author or the publishers. It is recommended that adults supervise children on the Internet.

Contents

Some words are printed in bold, **like this**. You can find out what they mean by looking in the Glossary.

Africa

Africa is the world's second largest **continent**, covering roughly 11.5 million square miles (30 million square kilometers). Several islands lie off the coast, including Madagascar.

Africa has many different types of landscapes. The Sahara Desert is in the north. It is the world's largest desert and it covers one-third of the continent. The **equator** crosses central Africa and **rain forests** grow here. To the east are rolling **grasslands**. There are also snow-capped mountains, and some of the world's longest rivers and largest lakes can be found in Africa.

The grasslands of East Africa are famous for their amazing animals.

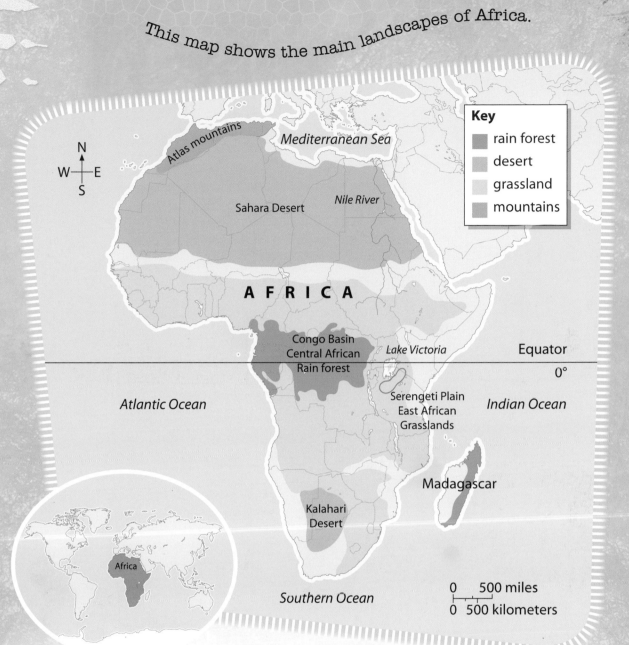

This map shows the main landscapes of Africa.

Key
- rain forest
- desert
- grassland
- mountains

N
W—E
S

Atlas mountains

Mediterranean Sea

Sahara Desert

Nile River

A F R I C A

Congo Basin
Central African
Rain forest

Lake Victoria

Equator
0°

Atlantic Ocean

Serengeti Plain
East African
Grasslands

Indian Ocean

Madagascar

Kalahari
Desert

Africa

0   500 miles
0 500 kilometers

Southern Ocean

An amazing range of animals live in the different landscapes. Huge herds of zebra and wildebeest roam the grassy plains. Hippos and crocodiles swim in rivers and **swamps**. Flamingos and other birds flock to the lakes to nest and feed. Chimpanzees and gorillas live in the rain forests. These animals have special features that help them survive in their specific **habitats**.

5

Savannah Elephant

The Savannah elephant is the world's largest land animal. It is a **mammal**. Its body is designed for feeding on the grasses and plants that grow in its **grassland** habitat.

Elephant food

The elephant changes what it eats when the seasons change. In the wet season it mainly eats grasses since there are plenty of them. In the dry season the grasses die. Then the elephant eats bark, twigs, flowers, fruits, and roots.

Savannah elephants use their huge ears as fans to cool down their bodies.

Body design

An elephant's skull, jaws, and teeth allow it to eat hard plants. The tusks are actually very long front teeth. The elephant uses them for stripping bark from trees and digging up roots. An elephant also has large teeth inside its mouth for grinding food. An elephant's trunk is really its nose. It uses it to smell and also to pick up food.

where savannah elephants live

Africa

Atlantic Ocean

Indian Ocean

Southern Ocean

Elephants need to eat about 330 lbs (150 kg) of food a day.

Cheetah

On the **grasslands**, cheetahs hunt animals, such as small antelopes. The cheetah starts by **stalking** its **prey**. It hides among the tall, dry grass. When it is close enough to its prey, it suddenly chases.

CHEETAH

BODY LENGTH:
UP TO 5 FT. (1.5 M)

TAIL LENGTH:
UP TO 33 IN. (85 CM)

WEIGHT:
88–143 LBS (40–65 KG)

LIFESPAN:
UP TO 12 YEARS

HABITAT:
GRASSLAND AND SEMI-DESERT

THAT'S AMAZING!:
CHEETAH CUBS SPEND MOST OF THEIR TIME PLAYING GAMES OF STALKING AND POUNCING. THIS IS A WAY OF PRACTICING FOR HUNTING WHEN THEY GROW UP.

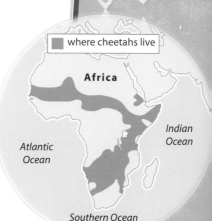

where cheetahs live

Africa

Atlantic Ocean

Indian Ocean

Southern Ocean

A cheetah can reach a top speed of 70 mph (114 kph).

A cheetah can only run for a short distance before it gets tired.

Built for speed

The cheetah, which is a **mammal,** is the fastest animal on land. Its slender body is built for speed. Its flexible backbone allows it to take giant leaps. Its claws grip the ground like spikes on a running shoe. A cheetah uses its tail for steering when it turns quickly after its prey.

Ostrich

Ostriches are the world's largest, heaviest, and tallest birds. Males have black and white feathers. Females are grayish-brown. An ostrich cannot fly but has long, powerful legs for running fast. When it is in danger, an ostrich runs away. It can move as quickly as 45 mph (72 kph). It also uses its legs in self-defense. It can kick and slash with its sharp claws.

OSTRICH

HEIGHT:
5.7–8.8 FT.
(1.7–2.7 M)

WEIGHT:
UP TO 330
LBS (150 KG)

LIFESPAN:
50 YEARS

HABITAT:
GRASSLANDS; DESERTS

THAT'S AMAZING!:
OSTRICHES CAN LIVE WITHOUT WATER FOR A LONG TIME. THIS IS VERY USEFUL SINCE THEY LIVE IN DRY PLACES. THEY GET MOISTURE FROM THE PLANTS THEY EAT.

where ostriches live

Africa

Atlantic
Ocean

Indian
Ocean

Southern Ocean

Ostriches have two toes on their feet. Their toes help them to run fast.

Swallowing stones

Ostriches spend much of the day feeding. They eat whatever they can find in their **habitat**. This means mostly plants, especially roots, leaves, and seeds. But they also eat **insects** and small lizards. Ostriches do not have teeth for chewing food so they swallow stones, pebbles, and sand to help grind up their food.

An ostrich egg is very big. It is ten times bigger than a chicken egg.

Goliath Beetle

The goliath beetle is one of the largest **insects** in the world. Adults can weigh three times as much as a mouse. Goliath beetles eat sap and fruit from **rain forest** trees.

GOLIATH BEETLE

BODY LENGTH:
UP TO 6 IN. (15 CM)

WEIGHT:
2.4–3.5 OZ. (70–100 G)

LIFESPAN:
FEW MONTHS (ADULTS)

HABITAT:
RAIN FOREST

THAT'S AMAZING!:
GOLIATH BEETLES HAVE SHARP CLAWS AT THE END OF EACH LEG TO HELP THEM CLIMB TREES TO FEED.

where goliath beetles live

Africa

Atlantic Ocean

Indian Ocean

Southern Ocean

A male goliath beetle has a Y-shaped horn on its head.

Goliath beetles are so large that they make a noise like a mini helicopter when they fly.

Beetle life cycle

The life cycle of a goliath beetle is linked to the seasons of the rain forest. The beetle lays its eggs on the ground early in the rainy season. When the **larvae** hatch, they feed on rotting leaves and wood. Then they burrow in the ground and build a hard case of soil around them. Inside, their bodies change into adults. They stay in the ground until the dry season ends. When the rainy season begins again, they break out of their cases and search for a **mate**.

Gaboon Viper

The Gaboon viper is a large snake with brown, pink, and orange skin. It has diamond-shaped marks down its sides. This coloring gives it excellent **camouflage**. By the time the snake's **prey** spots the snake, it is too late to escape.

The snake's coloring makes it very difficult to spot on the rain forest floor.

Fangs and food

The Gaboon viper feeds on birds and small **mammals,** such as rats. It hunts for food at night. It waits for its prey to come near, then kills it with a bite. The bite is so poisonous that it can kill a small animal instantly. The viper does not only kill when it is hungry. It will also attack if it is threatened or disturbed.

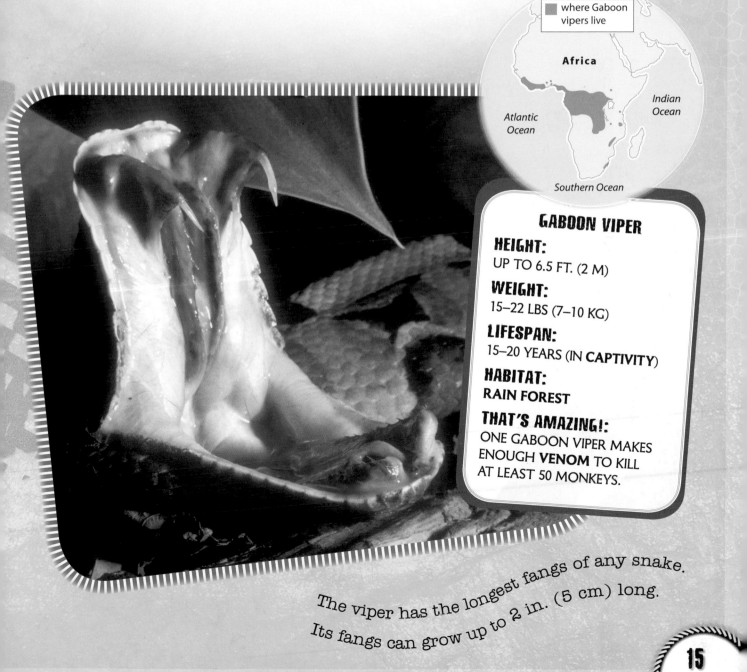

where Gaboon vipers live

Africa

Atlantic Ocean

Indian Ocean

Southern Ocean

GABOON VIPER

HEIGHT:
UP TO 6.5 FT. (2 M)

WEIGHT:
15–22 LBS (7–10 KG)

LIFESPAN:
15–20 YEARS (IN **CAPTIVITY**)

HABITAT:
RAIN FOREST

THAT'S AMAZING!:
ONE GABOON VIPER MAKES ENOUGH **VENOM** TO KILL AT LEAST 50 MONKEYS.

The viper has the longest fangs of any snake. Its fangs can grow up to 2 in. (5 cm) long.

Aye-Aye

The aye-aye is a small **mammal**. It has bat-like ears, big yellow eyes, and large front teeth. Its tail is long and bushy and its thick gray-brown coat is flecked with white. It lives high up in the trees of the **rain forest**.

AYE-AYE

HEIGHT:
12–16 IN. (30–40 CM)

TAIL LENGTH:
16–20 IN.
(40–50 CM)

WEIGHT:
4.5–6.5 LBS
(2–3 KG)

LIFESPAN:
UP TO 23 YEARS
(IN **CAPTIVITY**)

HABITAT:
RAIN FORESTS, DRY
FORESTS IN MADAGASCAR

THAT'S AMAZING!:
THE AYE-AYE SPENDS THE DAY
SLEEPING IN A NEST MADE FROM
LEAVES AND TWIGS, THEN GOES
OUT HUNTING AT NIGHT.

where aye-ayes live

Atlantic Ocean

Indian Ocean

Africa

Madagascar

Southern Ocean

The aye-aye's large eyes and ears help it to locate its **prey** at night.

Finger food

The aye-aye has very long, middle fingers that it uses for scooping out fruits and for finding **insect larvae**. The aye-aye taps on a tree branch and listens for hollow spaces where larvae might be found.

Madagascar
Madagascar lies off the southeast coast of Africa and is the world's fourth largest island. It is home to some of the most unusual wildlife on Earth. Roughly 80 percent of its animals, including the aye-aye, are found nowhere else in the world.

The aye-aye tears the wood open with its teeth and uses its finger to pull the grubs out.

Sociable Weaverbird

Sociable weaverbirds live in the dry desert. They rarely need to drink because they get moisture from the seeds and **insects** they eat.

Sociable weaverbirds are small, brown birds roughly the size of sparrows.

SOCIABLE WEAVERBIRD

BODY LENGTH:
5.4 IN. (14 CM)

WEIGHT:
0.9–1 OZ. (26–30 G)

LIFESPAN:
UP TO 5 YEARS

HABITAT:
DESERT

THAT'S AMAZING!:
A SOCIABLE WEAVERBIRD NEST CAN WEIGH SEVERAL TONS. IT CAN GET SO HEAVY THAT IT KNOCKS DOWN THE TREE IT IS BUILT ON.

where sociable weaverbirds live

Africa

Atlantic Ocean

Indian Ocean

Southern Ocean

The roof of the nest is made from large twigs. The chambers are built from dry grasses and lined with soft leaves or fur.

Nest building

Weaverbirds build enormous nests in the trees. A single nest may have **chambers** for up to 100 families. The nest keeps the birds comfortable in the tough desert climate. On cold nights, the cosy inner chambers keep the birds warm. On hot summer days the birds stay cool in chambers on the outside of the nest.

Desert Locust

The desert locust is a type of grasshopper. It lives in the desert and feeds on plants. It eats roughly its own weight in food each day. The locust is usually shy and lives alone, but all this changes if it starts to rain. The rain makes plants grow and this gives plenty of food for the locusts and their young. Then the locusts breed quickly and form enormous **swarms**.

Even a small swarm can contain roughly 50 million **insects**.

Locust swarms

The swarms of locusts can fly hundreds of miles a day, carried by the wind. They eat any plants they can find. A swarm of locusts can eat hundreds of thousands of tons of food in a day.

DESERT LOCUST

BODY LENGTH:
1.7–2.3 IN. (4.5–6 CM)

WEIGHT:
0.07 OZ. (2 G)

LIFESPAN:
3–5 MONTHS

HABITAT:
DESERTS

THAT'S AMAZING!:
LOCUSTS LAY UP TO 100 EGGS IN AN EGG POD IN THE SAND. THE FEMALE COVERS THEM WITH FOAMY FROTH TO KEEP THE EGGS FROM DRYING OUT.

where desert locusts live

Africa

Indian Ocean

Atlantic Ocean

Southern Ocean

Locusts destroy crops on farms.

Nile Crocodile

The Nile crocodile is one of the world's largest **reptiles**. The crocodile lies in the water waiting for its **prey**. Then it grabs its victim in its huge jaws and drags it beneath the water to drown it.

NILE CROCODILE

BODY LENGTH:
UP TO 20 FT. (6.1 M)

WEIGHT:
500 LBS (225 KG)

LIFESPAN:
45 YEARS

HABITAT:
RIVERS, LAKES, **SWAMPS**

THAT'S AMAZING!:
CROCODILES SOMETIMES HUNT IN GROUPS. THEY HERD FISH TOWARD THE BANK, THEN EAT THEM!

where Nile crocodiles live

Africa

Atlantic Ocean

Indian Ocean

Southern Ocean

A crocodile's gray-green coloring gives excellent **camouflage**.

This crocodile is waiting for prey.

Special features

Crocodiles have **adapted** well to life in the river. Their nostrils, eyes, and ears are on top of their heads so that they can breathe, see, and hear in the water.

The mother carries the babies in her mouth to the water for their first swim.

Eggs and babies

A female crocodile lays her eggs in a hole in the river bank and covers them with sand. Both parents guard the nest. When the baby crocodiles are ready to hatch, they make a chirping sound and the female digs up the eggs.

Lungfish

The lungfish is a fish with a long, snake-like body. It lives in shallow water in **swamps** and streams. Lungfish are fierce hunters and will eat anything they can catch. They mainly feed on frogs, small fish, and crabs.

Gills

In the wet season, lungfish breathe oxygen from the water through their **gills**.

Out of water

In the wet season, when there is plenty of water, lungfish live like normal fish. But in the dry season, their swamps and streams dry out. The lungfish have a special way of surviving. They dig burrows in the damp mud and curl up inside. Then they cover their bodies in slimy **mucus** to keep them from drying out. They can stay like this for many months until it rains again.

LUNGFISH

BODY LENGTH:
UP TO 6.5 FT. (2 M)

WEIGHT:
40 LBS (17 KG)

LIFESPAN:
10 YEARS (IN **CAPTIVITY**)

HABITAT:
SWAMPS AND STREAMS

THAT'S AMAZING!:
THE LUNGFISH BLOCKS THE ENTRANCE OF ITS BURROW WITH MUD. THE MUD KEEPS WATER OUT BUT LETS A SMALL AMOUNT OF AIR IN.

where lungfish live

Africa

Atlantic Ocean

Indian Ocean

Southern Ocean

Animals in Danger

Many animals in Africa are in danger of dying out forever. When an animal dies out, it is said to be **extinct**. Animals are dying out because people are destroying their **habitats**, capturing them for pets, or killing them for their skins, meat, and body parts.

The black rhinoceros is in danger of becoming extinct. Tens of thousands of rhinos have been killed for their horns. Today, there are fewer than 4,000 black rhinos left, mainly living in East and South Africa. In West Africa, they may already be extinct.

Rhino horns are used to make dagger handles and some types of **traditional medicine**.

There are only about 360 of these mountain gorillas left in the rain forests of Central Africa.

Another animal at risk is the mountain gorilla. Many gorillas have been shot for food or killed in the wars taking place in the region. Others, especially babies, have been captured and taken away to be pets. The forest habitat where the gorillas live is also in danger of disappearing. Large areas of forest are being chopped down to make way for farms.

Today, **conservation** groups are working hard to save these amazing animals.

Animal Facts and Figures

There are millions of different types of animals living all over the world. The place where an animal lives is called its **habitat**. Animals have special features, such as wings, claws, and fins. These features allow animals to survive in their habitats. Which animal do you think is the most amazing?

SAVANNAH ELEPHANT

BODY LENGTH:
13–16 FT. (4–5 M)

WEIGHT:
4.4–7.7 TONS

LIFESPAN:
60 YEARS

HABITAT:
GRASSLAND

THAT'S AMAZING!:
AN ELEPHANT'S TUSKS GROW THROUGHOUT ITS LIFE AND CAN REACH MORE THAN 10 FT. (3 M) LONG.

OSTRICH

HEIGHT:
5.7–8.8 FT. (1.7–2.7 M)

WEIGHT:
UP TO 330 LBS (150 KG)

LIFESPAN:
50 YEARS

HABITAT:
GRASSLANDS; DESERTS

THAT'S AMAZING!:
OSTRICHES CAN LIVE WITHOUT WATER FOR A LONG TIME. THIS IS VERY USEFUL SINCE THEY LIVE IN DRY PLACES. THEY GET MOISTURE FROM THE PLANTS THEY EAT.

CHEETAH

BODY LENGTH:
UP TO 5 FT. (1.5 M)

TAIL LENGTH:
UP TO 33 IN. (85 CM)

WEIGHT:
88–143 LBS (40–65 KG)

LIFESPAN:
UP TO 12 YEARS

HABITAT:
GRASSLAND AND SEMI-DESERT

THAT'S AMAZING!:
CHEETAH CUBS SPEND MOST OF THEIR TIME PLAYING GAMES OF STALKING AND POUNCING. THIS IS A WAY OF PRACTICING FOR HUNTING WHEN THEY GROW UP.

GOLIATH BEETLE

BODY LENGTH:
UP TO 6 IN. (15 CM)

WEIGHT:
2.4–3.5 OZ. (70–100 G)

LIFESPAN:
FEW MONTHS (ADULTS)

HABITAT:
RAIN FOREST

THAT'S AMAZING!:
GOLIATH BEETLES HAVE SHARP CLAWS AT THE END OF EACH LEG TO HELP THEM CLIMB TREES TO FEED.

GABOON VIPER

HEIGHT:
UP TO 6.5 FT. (2 M)

WEIGHT:
15–22 LBS (7–10 KG)

LIFESPAN:
15–20 YEARS (IN **CAPTIVITY**)

HABITAT:
RAIN FOREST

THAT'S AMAZING!:
ONE GABOON VIPER MAKES ENOUGH **VENOM** TO KILL AT LEAST 50 MONKEYS.

AYE-AYE

HEIGHT:
12–16 IN. (30–40 CM)

TAIL LENGTH:
16–20 IN. (40–50 CM)

WEIGHT:
4.5–6.5 LBS (2–3 KG)

LIFESPAN:
UP TO 23 YEARS (IN **CAPTIVITY**)

HABITAT:
RAIN FORESTS, DRY FORESTS IN MADAGASCAR

THAT'S AMAZING!:
THE AYE-AYE SPENDS THE DAY SLEEPING IN A NEST MADE FROM LEAVES AND TWIGS, THEN GOES OUT HUNTING AT NIGHT.

SOCIABLE WEAVERBIRD

BODY LENGTH:
5.4 IN. (14 CM)

WEIGHT:
0.9–1 OZ. (26–30 G)

LIFESPAN:
UP TO 5 YEARS

HABITAT:
DESERT

THAT'S AMAZING!:
A SOCIABLE WEAVERBIRD NEST CAN WEIGH SEVERAL TONS. IT CAN GET SO HEAVY THAT IT KNOCKS DOWN THE TREE IT IS BUILT ON.

DESERT LOCUST

BODY LENGTH:
1.7–2.3 IN. (4.5–6 CM)

WEIGHT:
0.07 OZ. (2 G)

LIFESPAN:
3–5 MONTHS

HABITAT:
DESERTS

THAT'S AMAZING!:
LOCUSTS LAY UP TO 100 EGGS IN AN EGG POD IN THE SAND. THE FEMALE COVERS THEM WITH FOAMY FROTH TO KEEP THE EGGS FROM DRYING OUT.

NILE CROCODILE

BODY LENGTH:
UP TO 20 FT. (6.1 M)

WEIGHT:
500 LBS (225 KG)

LIFESPAN:
45 YEARS

HABITAT:
RIVERS, LAKES, **SWAMPS**

THAT'S AMAZING!:
CROCODILES SOMETIMES HUNT IN GROUPS. THEY HERD FISH TOWARD THE BANK, THEN EAT THEM!

LUNGFISH

BODY LENGTH:
UP TO 6.5 FT. (2 M)

WEIGHT:
40 LBS (17 KG)

LIFESPAN:
10 YEARS (IN **CAPTIVITY**)

HABITAT:
SWAMPS AND STREAMS

THAT'S AMAZING!:
THE LUNGFISH BLOCKS THE ENTRANCE OF ITS BURROW WITH MUD. THE MUD KEEPS WATER OUT BUT LETS A SMALL AMOUNT OF AIR IN.

Find out more

Books to read

Ganeri, Anita. *Exploring Continents: Exploring Africa*. Chicago: Heinemann Library, 2007.

Parker, Steve. *Life Processes: Adaptation*. Chicago: Heinemann Library, 2007.

Parker, Steve. *Life Processes: Survival and Change*. Chicago: Heinemann Library, 2007.

Websites

http://animaldiversity.ummz.umich.edu
The Animal Diversity Web is run by the University of Michigan and features an extensive encyclopedia of animals.

http://animals.nationalgeographic.com/animals
This website features detailed information on various animals, stories of survival in different habitats, and stunning photo galleries.

http://www.bbc.co.uk/nature/reallywild
Type in the name of the animal you want to learn about and find a page with several facts, figures, and pictures.

http://www.mnh.si.edu
The website of the Smithsonian National Museum of Natural History, which has one of the largest natural history collections in the world.

Zoo sites
Many zoos around the world have their own websites that tell you about the animals they keep, where they come from, and how they are cared for.

Glossary

adapted when an animal has special features that help it to survive in its habitat

camouflage when an animal has special colors or markings that help it hide in its habitat

captivity animals kept in a zoo or wildlife park live in captivity. Animals in captivity often live longer than wild animals because they have no predators, nor is there competition for food.

chamber area like a room

conservation saving and protecting threatened animals and habitats

continent one of seven huge pieces of land on Earth. Each continent is divided into smaller regions called countries.

equator imaginary line running around the middle of the Earth

extinct when a type of animal dies out forever

gill part of a fish's body that is used for breathing in the water

grassland huge, open space covered in grass and bushes

habitat place where an animal lives and feeds

insect animal with six legs and three parts to its body

larvae grub-like young of insects

mammal animal that has fur or hair and feeds its babies milk

mate when an animal makes babies with another animal

mucus thick, slimy liquid

prey animals that are hunted and killed by other animals for food

rain forest thick forest growing around the equator where the weather is hot and wet

reptile animal with scaly skin that lays eggs on land

stalk move by creeping quietly

swamp area where large parts of the land are usually or always under water

swarm huge group of animals, such as insects

traditional medicine old-fashioned type of medicine

tropical places around the equator that are hot and wet all year round

venom another word for poison

Index